Elves and Fairies

Other titles in the Monsters and Mythical Creatures series include:

Aliens
Cyclops
Demons
Dragons
Frankenstein
Giants
Goblins
Medusa
The Mummy
The Sphinx
Trolls
Water Monsters
The Werewolf
Wizards
Zombies

Monsters
and Mythical Creatures

Elves and Fairies

Kris Hirschmann

ReferencePoint Press®

San Diego, CA

© 2013 ReferencePoint Press, Inc.
Printed in the United States

For more information, contact:
ReferencePoint Press, Inc.
PO Box 27779
San Diego, CA 92198
www.ReferencePointPress.com

LIBRARY OF CONGRESS CATALOGING-IN-PUBLICATION DATA

Hirschmann, Kris, 1967-
  Elves and fairies / by Kris Hirschmann.
    p. cm. -- (Monsters & mythical creatures)
  Includes bibliographical references and index.
  ISBN 978-1-60152-468-3 (hardback) -- ISBN 1-60152-468-4 (hardback) 1. Elves. 2. Fairies. I. Title.
GR549.H57 2013
  398.21--dc23
                                                              2012006965

Contents

All in the Family

Aclassic fairy encounter occurs early in *The Fellowship of the Ring*, the first book in J.R.R. Tolkien's *Lord of the Rings* trilogy. The hobbit Frodo Baggins and two friends, Pippin and Sam, set out on a journey. Almost immediately they encounter a group of elves trooping through the woods. Tolkien describes the moment in this passage: "Before long the Elves came down the lane towards the valley. They passed slowly, and the hobbits could see the starlight glimmering on their hair and in their eyes. They bore no lights, yet as they walked a shimmer, like the light of the moon above the rim of the hills before it rises, seemed to fall about their feet."[1]

> **Did You Know?**
>
> Elves and fairies are not immortal, but they have very long lives. They are believed to live for up to 400 years.

The elves and the hobbits proceed to pass the evening together. The hobbits spend much of this time in a blissful, elf-induced trance. As Tolkien relates:

> Pippin afterwards recalled little of either food or drink, for his mind was filled with the light upon the elf-faces, and the sound of voices so various and so beautiful that he felt in a waking dream. . . . Sam could never describe in words, nor picture clearly to himself, what he felt or thought that night, though it remained in his memory as one of the chief events of his life.[2]

These two passages give readers a glimpse at the looks and the enchanting powers of elves. Written in the mid-1900s, these words and the books in which they appear have become incredibly popular. They have played a key role in bringing elves to life in the modern imagination.

This does not mean, of course, that elves are Tolkien's invention. They are based on legends that originated thousands of years ago. In ancient Germanic mythology, elves were considered to be supernatural beings with distinct looks, personalities, and homes. They had magical powers that they could use to help—or hurt—human beings.

Meanwhile, across the waterway now called the English Channel, creatures called fairies were thought to populate the British Isles. Fairies were virtually identical to elves in concept. They differed a bit from their Germanic counterparts in their specific powers, habits,

With starlight glimmering in their hair and in their eyes, J.R.R. Tolkien's elves present an enchanting sight to the humble hobbits. Orlando Bloom plays the elf Legolas in the 2002 movie The Lord of the Rings: The Two Towers.

and appearances. But like elves, fairies were otherworldly beings that sometimes interacted with people. They could be helpful or harmful, depending on the circumstances.

So elves and fairies started out as distinct creatures. Somewhere along the line, though, Germanic elves crept into the British consciousness. They quickly carved out a home in the fairy pantheon, and by the 1500s elves were firmly and forever established as a type of fairy. As folklorists Brian Froud and Alan Lee explain, "'Elf-land' and 'Faerieland,' 'Elf' and 'Faerie' were and still are interchangeable words."[3]

This connection can be frustrating to people who care about strict divisions. Beings that are called *elves* in one source become *fairies* in another, and vice versa. To the casual observer, though, the combination offers endless opportunities for delight. All types of fairies, including elves, help people to connect with the enchantment and wonder that, some say, flow invisibly through the world. Mystical beings of all kinds are therefore portals to a world of truly magical possibilities.

Did You Know?

The English word *fairy* comes from the French *faei* or *fee*. Legends sometimes refer to fairies as *fay*.

Chapter 1

Defining Elves and Fairies

Creatures resembling elves and fairies populate the folklore of practically every time and culture. These beings pop up in the tales of ancient India, Persia, Iceland, China, North America, South America, and just about everywhere else human civilization has flourished. Variously friendly, dangerous, lovely, and hideous, these supernatural entities have long been considered a very real, if hidden, part of the natural world.

This is especially true in Europe, where elves and fairies have been part of the public consciousness for thousands of years. The traditions of this region abound with mystical creatures. By studying these traditions it is possible to paint a very clear picture of fairies' and elves' origins, looks, personalities, habits, and abilities.

What Are Fairies?

Fairies (sometimes spelled *faeries*) are human-like but supernatural beings with magical powers. These creatures go by many names, including the Little People, the Wee Folk, and the Gentle Folk. Like people, fairies differ considerably in their looks and behavior, their likes and dislikes. These tendencies are described at length in the lore of England, Wales, Scotland, and Ireland, where the Western fairy tradition originated.

There are many different accounts of the origin of fairies. The simplest explanation, perhaps, is that they are ghosts. According to this belief, a person's soul may linger on or near the mortal plane after death. This spirit becomes a fairy with newfound looks and powers. It can interact with the human world if it chooses, and it can even be a valuable guide to its still-living loved ones.

Other theories suggest that fairies have a divine origin. Early Christianity, for example, explained fairies as fallen angels. According to this view, many small spirits accidentally tumbled out of Heaven when the archangel Michael ejected Satan and his followers. When God closed Heaven's gates, these spirits were stranded outside. They embarked on a new existence as fairies, populating the trees, mountains, lakes, and fields where they had fallen.

A slightly different story holds that the fairies' fall from Heaven was no accident. It is said that God told all heavenly beings to choose between good and evil. Some angels chose good and stayed at God's side. Others chose evil and were cast into Hell. The ones who could not decide were ejected from Heaven to live on Earth. One scholar neatly sums up this concept in a major work about fairies. "Between good and evil, the archangel and the devil, legend discovers one being. This being is the Faerie,"[4] he says.

This view has been popular among various Christian sects. It has not, however, been universally accepted. Many people have preferred to think of fairies as the guardians of the natural world. Called by one author "the inner nature of the land and a reflection of the inner nature of our souls,"[5] fairies have often been considered the spirits of trees, water, weather, and other natural objects and forces. Still popular today, this idea sums up the essence of fairies for many believers.

What Are Elves?

Today, elves are considered a specific type of fairy. These beings originated in ancient Norse and Germanic mythology. It is said that they were born after the god Odin slew Ymir, the ice giant. Ymir's rotting corpse eventually produced maggots that squirmed out of the giant's

flesh. Odin saw these worms and separated them into two groups based on their color. The light-colored worms became the light elves, which were friendly and happy. The dark-colored worms became the dark elves, which were vicious and ill-natured.

In a classic 1835 work titled *Teutonic Mythology*, scholar Jacob Grimm (one of the brothers best known for their collection of fairy tales known today as *Grimm's Fairy Tales*) summarized the essential nature of ancient Germanic elves.

Apart from deified and semi-divine natures there stands a whole order of other beings distinguished mainly by the fact that, while those have issued from men or seek human fellowship, these form a separate community, one might say a kingdom of their own, and are only induced by accident or stress of circumstances to have dealings with men. . . . Their figure is much below the stature of man, or else mis-shapen.[6]

A fairy sparkles in the otherworldly darkness of a dense forest in Midsummer Night, *a painting by the nineteenth-century artist John Atkinson Grimshaw. Fairies come and go without warning in many tales but nearly always appear as glistening entities in mist or darkness.*

Fairies of the Sea

Many people think of fairy folk as creatures of the land and air. Folklorists, however, include many water-dwelling beings in the fairy category. Some well-known examples include undines, mermaids, selkies, banshees, and kelpies.

- **Undines.** Undines are elemental water spirits. They are said to inhabit every body of water, from the smallest stream to the greatest ocean. Undines are invisible to the human eye, but they are usually thought to be female, delicate, and beautiful. They have magical control over their watery environments.

- **Mermaids.** From the waist up, mermaids look like human women. Their lower bodies take the shape of thick, scaly fish tails. The mermaids of tradition are dangerous creatures whose singing lures sailors to their deaths.

- **Selkies.** Selkies are fairy folk who live in the seas surrounding the Orkney and Shetland Isles. They are human-like in their watery homes, but they take the shape of seals when they emerge from the sea. Selkies sometimes shed their seal skins when they interact with humans.

- **Banshee.** Traditionally spelled *beansidhe*, the banshee wails to warn of approaching human deaths. She usually appears as a washerwoman, cleaning filthy shrouds along the banks of rivers and streams.

- **Kelpies.** Kelpies are horse-like water fairies of Irish and Scottish lore. These creatures lure humans onto their backs, then carry their riders out to sea. They drown or eat their victims once they are far from land.

In the same book Grimm also examines the relationship between elves and dwarfs, another mythical race of Germanic origin. The scholar explains that, according to tradition, these beings are not the same. Various sources do, however, use elf-related words and names when talking about dwarfs. This fact leads Grimm to conclude that the Germanic term *âlfr* ("elf") could "shrink and stretch by turns."[7] In other words, it could apply to different beings under different circumstances.

Other Well-Known Fairies

This situation changed as time went by. Over the centuries most types of fairies, including elves, became more strictly defined. Today people recognize countless fairy "species," each with its own specific looks, powers, and habits.

The flower fairies are probably the best known of these varieties. Flower fairies are said to be tiny, slender, and childlike. They often have wings that they use to flit from one pretty bloom to another. They are irresistibly drawn to gardens, and although they are not often seen, their effects are evident. Their ceaseless work brings color and variety to flower patches everywhere.

Similar to flower fairies are the pixies. These beings are particularly well known in Cornwall, England, where scholars think they may have originated. Pixies are small and slender, with elf-like faces and pointed ears. They usually wear green outfits and pointed caps. They inhabit lonely moors but often approach populated areas. They especially love to borrow people's horses and take them for nighttime jaunts. They tangle the horses' hair as they ride, returning their mounts with filthy, matted manes.

The leprechaun is another trickster. Fairies of Irish folklore, these beings resemble very small, old men. They are always dressed crisply in green jackets, trousers, and hats. A leprechaun spends its time making tiny shoes and hoarding a stash of gold coins, which he hides at the end of a rainbow. Leprechauns can grant human wishes, if they choose—but usually they do not. These fairies are well known for making promises that they gleefully fail to keep.

More dependable by far is the brownie, an elf-like creature that appears in Scottish, Scandinavian, Slavic, and German folklore. Brownies are small, solitary fairies that often choose to live, unseen, with human families. They perform household tasks in exchange for small gifts. In the early 1700s author John Brand described this arrangement: "Every family had a *Brouny* . . . which served them, to which they gave a sacrifice for his service; as when they churned their milk, they took a part thereof, and sprinkled every corner of the house with it, for Brounie's use."[8]

This type of offering has to be made faithfully. If it is not, unpleasant consequences invariably ensue. At best, a disgruntled brownie might simply abandon its family. At worst, he might pinch sleeping family members, break household items, or perform other types of mischief. Brownies are therefore a burden as well as a boon to their human hosts.

Mystical Abodes

Brownies, hobgoblins, and a handful of other fairies may share people's houses. Most fairies, however, keep themselves separate from humans and their dwellings. They have their own mystical realms and haunts, many of which are identified in fairy legend and lore.

A place called Alfheim, or sometimes Elfhame, is one such spot. Loosely translated as "Elfland," Alfheim is the home of the light elves in Norse mythology. Ancient literature contains very few details about this realm, but at least one source mentions its abundance of beautiful residents. "The land governed by King Alf was called Alfheim, and all his offspring are related to the elves. They were fairer than any other people,"[9] states one ancient Norse text.

The same can be said of Faerieland, a realm very similar to Alfheim. Faerieland, or simply "Faerie," is basically the British version of Alfheim. It is an otherworldly place that exists on an alternate plane, one that humans can see only in fleeting glimpses. As authors Brian Froud and Alan Lee explain, "Faerie can reveal itself, bright and glittering without warning, anywhere and just as suddenly disappear. Its frontiers of twilight, mists and fancy are all around us and, like a tide running out, can momentarily reveal Faerie before flowing back to conceal it again."[10]

These magical moments are more likely to occur in some spots than in others. Great Britain, for instance, is supposedly ringed with islands where fairies lurk. Tir Nan Og, which lies somewhere off the Irish coast, is one of these places. Avalon, where the legendary King Arthur is said to lie today in a deep sleep, is another. Humans supposedly can visit these places—if they can find them. This quest is tricky, though, because these mystical islands do not appear on any map. Fairy guidance is usually needed when making this journey.

Closer by far are a handful of fairy-related natural objects. Fallen oaks, thorn trees, flowers, mushrooms, toadstools, and even some lakes are all thought to be fairy haunts. In Ireland certain earthen mounds are also said to hold fairies. All of these places act as links between the mortal and nonmortal worlds. They are excellent spots, it is said, to catch glimpses of the fairy realm.

Fairy Society

These moments may be brief. Still, they are revealing. Each fleeting glimpse of Faerieland gives people information about the beings that live therein.

Some of this information concerns fairy lifestyles. Observation suggests that some types of fairies live in societies that are governed by mystical kings, queens, and other royalty. Elves, which have highly developed customs and bow to one powerful king, live in this manner. So do the Daoine Sidhe (pronounced "Theena Shee") of Ireland and the Seelie Court of Scotland. The latter two groups are sometimes called trooping fairies because they like to "troop" together in solemn horseback processions. Called *rades*, these displays give humans the rare chance to see fairy society in action.

Not all fairies are so social. Many prefer to keep to themselves. Beings who follow this lifestyle are known as solitary fairies. Solitary fairies can be domestic, which means they live in or near human abodes. Brownie and flower fairies are two well-known examples that fall into this category.

Fairy Rings

Many legends speak of fairy rings. These flattened circles of grass are said to be places where otherworldly beings have danced the night away. This tale has a basis in reality. Dead patches *do* appear regularly in the fields and meadows of the British Isles. These patches are round, more or less, and their edges are sometimes ringed with neat rows of mushrooms. Fairy rings are so perfect, so precise, that it is easy to see why ancient people might have thought they had a supernatural origin.

Modern scientists, however, offer a different explanation. They explain that fairy rings get their start as underground fungi. These growths are not visible from above. Beneath the grass, though, the fungi are multiplying and spreading outward in a circular pattern. They rob the soil of essential nutrients as they travel. The grass above dies as a result, creating the classic trampled look of the fairy circle.

At the same time, the underground fungus is getting bigger and stronger. Eventually it is able to send shoots into the open air. These shoots occur only at the edges of the fungus patch, where the soil is not yet robbed of its nutrients. The shoots soon turn into a ring of mushrooms. Mushrooms grow very quickly, so these rings can spring up overnight— much to the confusion of those who do not understand their scientific origin.

Solitary fairies can also be nondomestic, which means they want nothing at all to do with humans or even with each other. They settle in remote areas where they will not be disturbed. As one folklorist puts it, these beings "rather like hermits, live far from human and other contact."[11] The leprechaun seems to be the least threatening member of this group. Other solitary fairies, such as the fearsome Pooka, the banshee, the water horse, the Leanhaun Shee (fairy mistress), and others, are much more monstrous. It is best to stay far away from areas where these beings are said to lurk.

Many Shapes, Sizes, and Looks

Different types of fairies are not distinguished merely by their lifestyles. They also look different. Each fairy race has physical features that distinguish it from its otherworldly relatives.

A fairy's height is one particularly telling feature. Fairies can be any size, from tiny to the size of a person—or even larger. Some flower fairies, for example, can sit comfortably within a blossom's petals. Brownies and leprechauns are larger, not quite reaching an adult human's waist. Elves, which approach or exceed human height, are among the tallest members of the fairy realm.

Fairies vary wildly in their looks as well as their size. Elves are thought to be among the most attractive of the fairy folk. One modern source offers the following description of these beings:

Both sexes usually have big, expressive eyes (in the most splendid colors). They wear their hair uncut and open, have graceful, fragile features and are of extraordinary beauty. Male elves also don't have any beard growth. Very typical for elves are their pointed ears, and high cheekbones. Some tribes are especially well known for their very exotic looking long necks, while other tribes have marvelous hair colors, ranging from silver to gold, to a variety of strangely glimmering, undefineable colors.[12]

This description paints a pleasant picture. Not all fairy folk, however, are so appealing. Dwarfs, for instance, are wrinkled, hunched, and dirty. Author Francis Melville describes goblins as "short and ugly to the point of hideousness."[13] Still other beings resemble demons or terrifying animals. Physical traits like these make some fairies very intimidating to human observers.

The opposite is true of wings, another feature that distinguishes certain fairy folk. Delicate, insect-like wings are especially characteristic of the flower fairies, which use their sparkling appendages to flit from one bloom to another. Beings called nymphs are often depicted with wings as well. Usually attractive, small, and gentle, winged fairies seem to be among the most approachable creatures in all of Faerie.

An Ever-Changing Appearance

"Seem to be," however, may be the key part of this description. Fairy folk are said to have a magical power called "glamour," which they can use to change their appearance at will. A fairy can thus seem dainty and sweet one moment, tall and terrible the next. As one child-sized being reportedly told an Irish peasant, "I am bigger than I appear to you now. We can make the old young, the big small, the small big."[14]

This is assuming, of course, that a fairy chooses to appear at all. Wee Folk of all types can make themselves visible or invisible to humans whenever they like. Different types of fairies have different preferences in this regard. Some allow themselves to be seen quite often, but others stay hidden as much as possible. Brownies, for example, never appear willingly and are visible only to those with psychic abilities. "[They] appeared only at night, . . . never allowing themselves to be seen by mortals. No person, except those gifted with second sight, could see the 'Brownies,'"[15] explains one writer.

Magical Abilities

Fairy magic goes much further than a few makeover tricks. Just as they can change their own appearance, fairies can also alter the looks of objects, places, and living beings. They are notorious, for instance, for handing out rocks and leaves disguised as gold coins. They can make a barren cave or a weed-filled meadow seen like a sumptuous palace. They can even transform people. Legends tell of fairies making ugly people beautiful—or, sometimes, the reverse. More than one young, attractive person is said to have become old and hideous at an angry fairy's hands.

Along with these transformative powers, fairies have many additional magical abilities. Some fairies, such as the leprechaun, are reputedly able to grant wishes. Others can bestow gifts of lifelong

Flower fairies are often portrayed in literature and art as having delicate wings resembling those of insects. Nineteenth-century artist John Anster Fitzgerald depicts them this way in Fairies Round a Bird's Nest.

luck or wealth. Still others use their magical powers to perform supernatural feats. In the classic tale of "Rumpelstiltskin," for instance, a wizened fairy creature helps an imprisoned girl by spinning straw into gold—an impossible task that no mere mortal could accomplish.

Equally magical is the fairy's ability to control nature. Some fairies can harness wind, water, or other aspects of the weather. Some can make flowers bloom or crops wither. Fairies also have a strong link with animals, which, says one author, "obey straightforward and help them in various tasks. . . . In the air, the elves may ask any bird to transport them across long distances."[16]

Fairy Personalities

This close link with nature comes across in the fairy personality. Like natural forces, fairy folk tend to be highly changeable. They can be cheerful and friendly one instant, spiteful and angry the next—and then recover their good moods just as quickly. In short, there is no telling what a fairy might do or say from one moment to the next.

Despite this essential changeability, it is possible to make certain generalizations about the fairy folk. Most types of fairies are fun-loving and mischievous. They like a good prank and will go to great lengths to tease their kin or, more often, any humans that venture nearby. Fairies also tend to be very curious. They will investigate anything unusual they see or hear. If they like what they find, they may impulsively join in the fun.

Fairies do not need outside interaction, however, to have a good time. They can find plenty of revelry among their own kind. Most fairies are skilled musicians, and they love to create tunes together. They also adore dancing. It is said that fairies enjoy all-night dance parties where groups circle a central point until they are too exhausted to continue. In the morning the fairies are gone, but the grass on which they danced is broken and flattened. Called fairy rings, these marks are said to be the visible evidence of fairy folk at play.

Not all fairies carouse in this way, of course. Some types of mystical beings are hardworking and serious. Dwarfs, for example, prefer to stay underground and tend to their mining and metal-working duties. Brownies and other types of house elves stay busy all night long with household chores. Leprechauns labor all day, every day cobbling tiny shoes. With so much work to do, these fairies and others have little time or inclination for merrymaking.

Good Versus Evil

Fairy folk differ in more ways than just their habits. Their essential natures vary as well. Folklore tells of good fairies, bad fairies, and downright evil fairies.

Some of these divisions occur within larger groups. The ancient Germanic elves, for instance, were split into the "good" light elves and the "evil" dark elves. The good elves lived in the pleasant land of Alfheim. The evil elves lurked underground in a sinister place called Svartálfaheimr. There are few details about these beings in ancient sources, but one author does say that they looked different. The light elves were "fairer than the sun to look at," whereas the dark elves were "blacker than pitch."[17]

A similar division between good and evil exists among the fairies of Scottish folklore. According to this tradition, good fairies of many different types were members of a society called the Seelie Court. Although these fairies were unpredictable, they were generally friendly and helpful to humans. They sometimes repaid human kindnesses with fairy favors or gifts.

At the opposite end of the spectrum were the evil fairies of the Unseelie Court. These malicious beings often attacked humans for no reason at all. They sometimes roamed together at night in bands called hosts, looking for lone travelers to torment. Bogeys, bogles, and boggarts were a few members of this unsavory group.

The lines between good and evil are not always so clearly drawn. Most traditions recognize a host of fairy types and individuals, each

Did You Know?

Some fairies lack solid bodies, seeming to be made out of light. Other fairies have a distinct odor that gives away their presence.

with its own tendency to help or hurt humans. Pixies, flower fairies, and brownies, for example, are generally good. Various types of goblins, on the other hand, cannot resist making mischief wherever they go. They have been known to throw objects, make incessant noise, and pinch mortal victims. They are also notorious for tormenting human miners with odd noises and deceptions.

These actions are undeniably annoying. But they could be worse—*much* worse. The most terrifying fairies do not stop at mere mischief. Instead, they try to destroy any humans they encounter. River fairies named Peg Powler and Jenny Greenteeth, for example, appear in English folklore. They love to seize passing children and drag them underwater. A snakelike Greek fairy called the Lamia is said to feed on children. She attacks babies in their beds, sucking out their blood and leaving empty husks behind.

Are Fairies and Elves Real?

This type of tale has been terrifying people for millennia. In the same way, stories of good fairies have enchanted listeners and readers. In both instances people of many times and many places have come to firmly believe that fairies truly exist.

Those who hold this belief point to items that, they say, are evidence of fairy activities. One such item is a tiny shoe discovered in Ireland in 1835. The shoe is less than 3 inches (8cm) long and is worn down at the heel, just as a full-size shoe would be if a person wore it for several years. Made of mouse skin and bearing tiny hand stitches, this object is said by some to be a leprechaun's work.

This shoe is not the only alleged fairy-made object that has been discovered by humans. People have also found fairy-sized pipes, coats, arrowheads, and even food. Believers claim that these objects were created and then lost by otherworldly beings. They say these things are proof that the fairy realm does, indeed, exist.

But other people scoff at this idea. They say that no one really knows how so-called fairy objects were created, and that a skilled human craftsperson can make just about anything. They also point out that no one has ever found a fairy's body or even a piece of a body. There is no hard evidence, they say, that fairy folk are now or have ever been real.

This argument, however, does not convince true believers. People have always felt a strong tie to elves and all the other residents of the fairy realm. Just because one cannot see the Little Folk, these people say, does not mean they are not there. In the hearts and minds of many people, fairies are just as real today as they have been for thousands of years.

Chapter 2

Encounters with the Little People

Fairies and mortals are said to live on separate planes of existence. These planes, however, must be closely connected because world folklore is rife with tales of human/fairy interactions. The Wee Folk can apparently pop into and out of the human realm at will to make trouble, to bestow gifts, to seek mortal spouses, and for countless other reasons.

Hundreds of years ago these encounters were taken for granted. As folklorist Janet Bord says, people of this time "knew that other levels of existence interacted with our own, and they had evolved rules for dealing with this interaction."[18] These rules were not formal. They were implied in tales that described how, when, why, and where people tended to encounter the Little People as well as the many curious things that took place during these events.

Seeing the Little Folk

All fairy/human encounters begin with a moment of discovery—an instant when a person comes face-to-face with an otherworldly being. Some types of people seem to be more likely than others to experience these moments.

A young girl finds herself surrounded by dancing fairies. Children are more open to the existence of fairies than adults and so are more likely to encounter them.

It appears that children are especially open to the fairy world. This is probably because young people do not question their senses the way adults do. A child who spots a fairy immediately knows that the "vision" is a supernatural being. Rather than being afraid, most children are delighted with their discovery and approach the fairy being as a potential playmate. Fairies adore this accepting attitude and will romp with children all day long, basking in their friendly regard.

By the time they are adults, most people have learned to block this type of experience. They ignore or reject things they do not understand. Fairies therefore escape their conscious notice. This veil can slip, however, when people enter a state of deep concentration. Absorbed in their own thoughts and feelings, people become more receptive to the natural world—and they may see fairies as a result. This type of encounter is especially common when people travel alone through stretches of remote countryside. The moment a traveler becomes lost in thought, fairy folk may appear.

This is most likely to occur, of course, in places where fairies typically lurk. Elves and all other types of fairies have their preferred hills, trees, woods, lakes, and other haunts. Humans who approach these places, either knowingly or unknowingly, are essentially trespassing on fairy territory.

Fairies usually take no action when these trespasses occur. They stay hidden and let the person pass. If a traveler is particularly interesting or irritating, however, a fairy may choose to appear.

Etiquette and Expectations

The nature of the encounter that follows depends mostly on the human's behavior. Fairies live by a code of strict etiquette, and they expect people to follow this code. They take great offense if their expectations are violated, and they may abandon or even punish mortals who do not meet their standards.

Strict honesty is one of these standards. Fairies expect humans to tell the truth at all times, even if the truth is uncomfortable. They become enraged if they discover they are being lied to. They will take revenge, if possible, on the human who uttered the untruth.

Secrecy is another requirement when dealing with fairy folk. Fairies may appear to humans and even help them in various ways, but they consider these arrangements to be private. They will abruptly cease their aid if a person shares the reason for his or her good luck.

A story from Wales illustrates this idea. The tale tells of a man who found silver fairy coins lying on the ground near his home each day. The man kept quiet about this good fortune for a long time. When his wife begged to know the source of the money, however, the man finally explained the situation. Lo and behold, the coins did not appear the following morning—or ever again. They had disappeared along with the fairies' goodwill.

This goodwill can also vanish, strangely enough, if a fairy is thanked for its services. It seems that fairies love to be appreciated but hate to be rewarded. This is particularly true of the brownies and other household fairies, who may abandon their human families in a huff if they are openly acknowledged. These Wee Folk do like and even expect gifts of food and drink, but only if they are left out "by accident." Explicit recognition is not welcomed or tolerated.

The worst offense of all is to give human clothing to a fairy. No one is sure why this act upsets fairies so much. Folkorist Brian Froud, however, believes that clothing carries implications people do not consider. "Nakedness, in the faery realm, is considered a highly honorable state. . . . The faeries will always resist attempts to impose human rules and mores on them. They ask . . . [that] we take them as they are—and thus a gift of clothes . . . can be misconstrued as a crude attempt to bind or control them,"[19] he explains.

Gifts and Rewards

It is undeniably hard for humans to live up to fairies' high and sometimes confusing standards. Folklore suggests, however, that the effort is well worthwhile. Fairies can be very generous when they approve

> **Did You Know?**
>
> The illness tuberculosis was once blamed on fairies. People who suffered from this disease, it was said, were wasting away from dancing with fairy folk all night.

The Cottingley Fairies

In the early 1900s two young girls caused a sensation by taking photos that seemed to show them playing with fairies. The Cottingley Fairies incident, as the uproar came to be known, began in 1917 at the home of 16-year-old Elsie Wright. Wright and her 10-year-old cousin, Frances Griffiths, claimed that the cottage's back garden was full of fairies. They borrowed a camera and took two pictures that seemed to prove this claim.

The girls' photos soon attracted attention. They were shown at a convention hosted by the Theosophical Society, an organization that encouraged belief in all manner of mythical creatures. A swirl of controversy immediately ensued. Some people believed that the photos were real. Others were convinced that the girls had faked the pictures. Meanwhile, Elsie and Frances swore they were telling the truth—and they produced three more fairy pictures to back up their story.

The Cottingley Fairies debate raged for decades. Throughout everything, the cousins stuck to their story. In 1983, however, the now elderly women made a confession: They had faked everything. They had traced pictures of fairies from a book and pinned them to trees and bushes. Then they had taken photos of themselves with the cutouts.

Despite this confession, Elsie continued to swear that the fairies had been real. Yes, she and her cousin had staged the photographs—but they really *had* played with otherworldly beings in the Cottingley garden. Whatever the truth may be, there is no doubt that the Cottingley Fairies story ranks among history's best-known fairy encounters.

of a person's behavior. They often reward kindness, good deeds, or talent with money, good luck, or other magical gifts.

Unfortunately for people who fall short of the mark, the reverse is also true. Fairies become very disgruntled when they are treated in ways they do not like. In these cases fairies may punish the offending human with physical afflictions, bad luck, perpetual poverty, or other terrible consequences.

In a compendium of fairy tales, folklorist Andrew Lang relates a story that describes both situations. "Toads and Diamonds" tells of a widow with two daughters. One day the younger daughter meets an old woman who begs for a drink of water. When the girl gladly complies, the fairy is pleased and bestows a gift. "At every word you speak, there shall come out of your mouth either a flower or a jewel,"[20] the fairy declares.

Upon seeing this gift, the girl's older sister becomes fiercely jealous. She seeks and finds the fairy, hoping to obtain the same gift for herself. But the sister displeases the fairy with her rudeness—and she reaps an awful reward for her behavior. "At every word you speak there shall come out of your mouth a snake or a toad,"[21] the fairy declares.

The results of this affliction are extreme, as is typical in folktales. The rude sister is thrown out of the house by her mother. Unable to find lodging, she eventually takes to the woods and dies. This sad situation does not seem to concern the fairy, however, because she never reappears or offers the girl a chance to redeem herself. It seems that angry fairies act impulsively, then continue on their way. The fairies' victims are left to cope with the lifelong consequences of their own thoughtlessness.

Making Mischief

Fairy mischief is not always the result of a person's actions. Sometimes fairies toy with humans simply because they feel like it. These interactions begin unexpectedly and can continue for hours or, in the most extreme cases, for years. They are endlessly frustrating to the human victims who experience them.

One well-known type of fairy mischief is the tendency to lead travelers astray. The pixies of Cornwall and Ireland are especially fond of this trick. For this reason, fairy misdirection is commonly known as being "pixy led." Pixy-led mortals suffer from mental confusion that stops them from going the right way. For instance, they might have trouble seeing a gate that is right in front of them, or they might find it impossible to follow a clear path. As folklorists Brian Froud and Alan Lee explain it, "A walker might abruptly find himself heading in a totally different direction to the way he wishes to go and no amount of re-alignment of his course seems to put this right."[22] The pixy-led individual will go helplessly back and forth until the fairy tires of its annoying game.

Misdirection is merely irritating. Other varieties of fairy mischief, however, are downright harmful. It is said that some types of fairy folk pinch humans in the night, an activity that leads to bruises, cramps, rheumatism, and other disorders. Different types of fairies, including elves, are said to cause deformities such as lame legs and hunched backs. In the most extreme cases, fairy interference can even kill. Unexplained infant deaths, heart attacks, and many other fatal conditions were once thought to be caused by spiteful fairy folk.

Tricked and Trapped

Not all fairies want to harm mortals. Many mystical beings seem to enjoy and even crave human company. They offer food, drink, merriment, music, and other enticements to lure people into their gatherings.

These gatherings, unfortunately, are fraught with peril. Humans who enter the fairy realm are in danger of being trapped. They can avoid this fate by refusing to eat or drink fairy refreshments. They also cannot accept fairy kisses. Any of these things will bind a mortal to the fairies for all eternity.

Fairy music also has binding powers. Many tales tell of travelers who stop to listen to fairies' tunes. When the music ends the mortal discovers that he has been listening, spellbound, for hours or even years. In the Welsh "Legend of Shon ap Shenkin," for example, a young man named Shon becomes mesmerized by a mystical melody. He listens for what seems to be a few minutes. When the music stops, the young man returns home—only to discover that many decades have passed. Now impossibly old, Shon crumbles to dust on his doorstep.

Fairy music has enchanting effects even when fairies themselves are not present. Scandinavian lore addresses this danger. As one story goes, "There is . . . a tune called the Elf-king's tune, which several of the good fiddlers know right well, but never venture to play, for as soon as it begins both old and young, and even inanimate objects, are impelled to dance, and the player cannot stop unless he can play the air backwards, or that some one comes behind him and cuts the strings of his fiddle."[23]

People also need outside help to escape from fairy dances. These dances occur in remote meadows and may involve hundreds of fairy folk prancing wildly in circles. The fairies love it when people join them—but like eating and drinking fairy food, this invitation is a trap. A person who steps into a fairy circle finds himself compelled to dance along with the Wee Folk. The revelry continues until someone yanks the dancer out of the circle or until he or she drops dead of exhaustion, whichever comes first.

> ## Did You Know?
> It is said that fairies sometimes use human captives to pay a tithe called *teind* to Hell. This payment is due once every seven years.

Stolen at Birth

In the case of fairy rings, it does not seem that the Little People are trying to hurt the humans they trap. They simply want to play, and they are totally indifferent to their mortal dance partners' wants, needs, and feelings.

The same lack of concern is evident in the fairy tendency to kidnap human babies. Fairies are irresistibly attracted to infants, especially those with golden hair. They often spirit these babies away to Faerieland and leave decoys, called changelings, in their place.

There are several types of changelings. One common type is a block of wood carved in the exact image of the missing child. The baby's parents are convinced that this wooden object is their infant, tragically dead. They bury the replica and go on with their lives, never suspecting that their child is actually alive and well in the fairy realm.

Fairies often leave living changelings behind as well. These creatures may be old, ugly elves or the fairies' own unwanted babies. A fairy uses its powers of glamour to disguise the imposter, but the illusion seems to slip over time. According to Froud and Lee, the changeling "may develop a wizened or deformed appearance, or be sickly and fretful, or else have a voracious appetite."[24] Any or all of these signs may lead people to wonder if their child is, in reality, a fairy changeling.

A parent who suspects the worst can sometimes trick fairies into returning a human child. Threatening to hurt or kill the changeling seems to be one effective method. In one Danish tale a mother prepares to destroy a changeling by shoving it into a hot oven. At the last possible moment, the story says, "[a] troll-woman came in a great fright with the real child, and took away her own, saying, 'There's your child for you. I have treated it better than you treated mine.'"[25] Restored to its rightful parents, the human baby was never again bothered by trolls or any other fairy beings.

Warding Off the Wee Folk

This story illustrates an important point about the fairy folk. They may be powerful and dangerous, but they can be thwarted with the right tricks and tools. Folk tradition describes many ways to protect oneself against ill-intentioned fairies.

The use of iron is said to be the best protection. Fairies are weakened by this metal, and some can even be killed by it. Fairy beings of all types therefore avoid humans who carry iron. A knife,

Elfin Mischief

Many human misfortunes have been attributed to elves. In their classic book *Faeries*, Brian Froud and Alan Lee discuss several such traditions. Sudden, unexplained deaths of animals and humans, for instance, "were believed to be due to 'Elf-shot.' Small flint arrowheads, which we now know were made by Stone-Age man, were attributed to the elves. Where no physical shot was in evidence it was assumed the arrowhead made no wound but instead induced paralysis. The victim could then be carried away to Faerie while a replica body was left behind to sicken and die."

Froud and Lee also explain that the affliction known today as a stroke originated in elfin beliefs. "'Stroke,' in the sense of paralytic seizure, is a word we still use, probably unaware that it originally meant 'Elf-stroke,'" they say. Fine one moment and senseless the next, stroke victims do seem like victims of some invisible evil. It is not hard to see how people with no medical knowledge might have blamed fairy folk for this sudden "stroke" of disaster.

More benign but still annoying is the elfin tendency to tangle human hair. Elves perform this mischief at night, when people are fast asleep. The resulting "elf-locks," as these tangles are known, are a daily irritation for men, women, and children everywhere.

Brian Froud and Alan Lee, "Faerie Ways," in *Faeries*. New York: Peacock/Bantam, 1978.

a pair of scissors, or even a nail in the pocket is sufficient to deter the fairy folk. Likewise, iron nails driven above a door or into a bed frame protect human homes and their residents from fairy interference.

Bells can have the same effect. Church bells, for instance, originated as a way of protecting worshippers from evil entities. The bells hung around the necks of sheep, oxen, and other farm animals were also meant to ward off fairies.

If no iron or bells are handy, perhaps a sandwich can do the job. Newfoundland tradition in particular holds that fairies dislike bread and will avoid it at all costs. In her classic book *An Encyclopedia of Fairies*, folklorist Katharine Mary Briggs expands upon this concept. "The prototype of food, and therefore a symbol of life, bread was one

A secret stash of gold is said to be the leprechaun's greatest and most closely guarded possession. According to legends, threats are the only way to learn the location of the leprechaun's treasure.

of the commonest protections against fairies. Before going out into a fairy-haunted place, it was customary to put a piece of dry bread in one's pocket,"[26] she says.

If bread were not available, many other items might do in a pinch. Various traditions mention the use of oatmeal, four-leaf clovers, Saint John's wort, daisies, rowan wood, and salt. Running water and fire might also discourage fairies from approaching.

Catching Mystical Creatures

Most humans do everything in their power to ward off elves and fairies. Some people, however, do just the opposite. They try to find and even imprison fairy folk. By doing so, they hope to obtain magical riches, blessings, or other boons.

Of all fairy folk, the leprechaun is undoubtedly the most sought after. Each leprechaun is said to have a secret stash of gold. A trapped leprechaun will reveal the gold's location if pressed, but extreme threats are usually required. "I pulled out a knife I'd in my pocket, an' put on as wicked a face as ivir I could . . . an' swore by this and by that, if he didn't instantly gi' me his purse, or show me a pot o' goold, I'd cut the nose aft his face,"[27] says a character in one Irish legend. The terrified leprechaun had no choice but to comply.

Money is not the only incentive to catch leprechauns. These beings can also grant wishes in return for their release. Leprechauns usually wiggle out of any such promises, but folklore shows that they do occasionally come through. An Irish king called Fergus mac Léti, for example, requested and received the ability to breathe underwater from a captive leprechaun.

Love Connections

Fairy folk are not pursued only for their magical favors. Sometimes people trap fairies because they love them and do not want them to return to the fairy realm.

Such is the case in the Welsh tale known as "The Fairy Wife." In this legend a young man spots a graceful fairy and falls head over heels in love. Under the impulse of this passion, says the tale, the man "snatched the lovely maiden in his arms, and ran off instantly with her into the house." Other fairies try to rescue their friend, but they cannot reach her because "the door was locked and bolted, and the stolen maiden was safely lodged in a chamber. The iron bolt and lock made it impossible for them to reclaim her, for the Fair Family abhor iron."[28]

In this particular story the human's quest is successful: The young man eventually wins his prisoner's love. In other stories, however, the results are different. Many tales tell of fairies pining for their homes and trying desperately to escape their human captors.

Such is the case in "The Legend of the Seal Woman." In this tale, which originated in the Faroe Islands between Scotland and Iceland, a man steals the pelt of a selkie (seal fairy) and locks the pelt in a chest. He forces the selkie, now trapped in human form, to marry him and bear several children.

The selkie endures this situation in misery for many years until one day the man forgets his chest key at home. The fairy wife retrieves her pelt and escapes to the sea. She returns one time to vow revenge against her former husband and neighbors, then disappears forever. Her enraged influence, however, is said to persist to this very day. "Bad news has come from [this region] way too often. Men have fallen from cliffs, when they have been in the mountains tending sheep or catching birds,"[29] says one modern account. Locals blame the Seal Woman for this continuing misfortune.

Modern Encounters

This type of belief is not unique to the Faroe Islands. It seems that people everywhere are still running into fairies on a regular basis. Folklorist Janet Bord addresses this curious fact in her in-depth study of fairy encounters. "To many people fairies exist only in fairy tales, but my research has shown me that many people . . . at the end of the twentieth century, are still seeing fairies. . . . Anyone who thinks fairies are a joke will be very surprised to learn how many first-hand sighting reports are in existence,"[30] she says.

Bord offers many examples to support her argument. She describes, for instance, a 1987 event that occurred in Yorkshire, England. Several people saw fairy-like figures dancing around a pole late at night. The figures disappeared when the people ran over to investigate. It was noted that the ground upon which the figures had danced was muddy—yet not a single footprint was left behind.

In the early 1990s another odd incident occurred. A teenage boy saw two small, elf-like figures fishing from a Scottish sea cliff. The little men vanished when the boy approached, leaving a tiny pipe behind. The boy took the pipe home as a souvenir and placed it in a locked drawer. When he looked for his treasure the next morning, however, it was gone. The elves had apparently retrieved their property in the middle of the night.

Stories like these keep the fairy mystique alive—and they also keep the old traditions running strong. In places where the Little Folk are still said to appear, many locals continue to follow the classic rules of human/fairy interaction. They may avoid fairy haunts, for instance, or they may build their houses in ways that accommodate the wishes and needs of their otherworldly neighbors. They may carry bits of iron or bread in their pockets. In a 1968 incident, an Irish construction crew even refused to cut down an alleged fairy tree. "I have heard so much about these fairy trees that I would not risk it,"[31] the foreman in charge of the job said later.

This attitude may seem extreme. To those who believe in fairies, though, it is simply prudent. The fairy folk are unpredictable at best and dangerous at worst. When it comes to human/fairy encounters, avoidance is the only sensible approach.

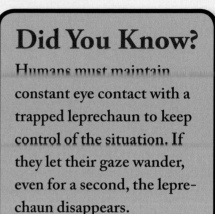

Did You Know?

Humans must maintain constant eye contact with a trapped leprechaun to keep control of the situation. If they let their gaze wander, even for a second, the leprechaun disappears.

Chapter 3

Elves and Fairies in Literature and Film

The idea of Faerieland has fascinated humans for thousands of years, and it is easy to see why. This mystical realm appears only in brief, unexpected flashes. It gives people the merest glimpse of its otherworldly residents and marvels, then disappears without a trace.

Brief though they may be, these glimpses—or reports of them, anyway—have been an endless source of inspiration to human storytellers of all places and ages. Fairy-related tales were passed down verbally long before most people knew how to read or write. In the earliest days of the written word, fairy beings started to pop up in literature and poetry. They inspired medieval books, plays, and fairy tales that are beloved even today.

Modern work reflects the fairy influence, too. Elves and their mystical kin romp through today's literature and films. These beings look and act a bit different from one source to the next. But in one sense, they are all the same: They are modern-day artists' efforts to bring ancient traditions to life.

Ancient Ballads

Some of the earliest fairy stories appeared in epic poems that are now called "border ballads." The poems got this name because they originated along the border between England and Scotland. Appearing at least 800 years ago, the border ballads covered topics that interested people of the time. One of these topics, of course, was the fairy folk.

A poem called "Tam Lin" is among the most famous of the border ballads. This story tells of Tam Lin, a human who is stolen by the queen of the fairies as a young boy. Tam Lin worries that the queen is preparing to sacrifice him to Hell as part of the fairies' seven-year tithe, and he begs a young woman to help him escape from this dread fate. The pair's plot succeeds and Tam Lin is freed—much to the dismay of the fairy queen, who loves her handsome prisoner. "She has ta'en away the bonniest knight in all my company,"[32] the queen wails in one version of the tale.

The ballad of "Thomas the Rhymer" offers a different take on the fairy abduction theme. In this story, a man named Thomas comes upon a stunningly beautiful woman whom he addresses as the queen of Heaven. The vision shakes her head and speaks:

"O no, O no, Thomas," she said,
"That name does not belang to me;
I am but the queen of fair Elfland,
That am hither come to visit thee."[33]

It turns out that the elf queen does not merely want to visit Thomas. She whisks the human away to Elfland, where he lives as a guest for seven years. Thomas returns to the mortal realm at the end of this period, but only briefly. Before long he voluntarily returns to Elfland to live forever with his fairy love.

Medieval Times

Human/fairy romance and other interactions provided continuing inspiration for storytellers as the centuries passed. The theme was especially popular in and immediately around the 1400s. During this period many writers employed mystical beings in works of fiction.

The tales of roving knights—known as "knights errant"—offer many examples of this use. Knights errant were armored soldiers who wandered about in search of adventure. Sometimes they encountered fairy folk during their travels. In the tale of Sir Launfal, for example, a knight meets and falls in love with the fairy queen Tryamour. The fairy pledges herself to Launfal, with one strict condition. "Make no boast of me for any reward; if you do, you shall lose all my love,"[34] she says. The rest of the tale follows the unfortunate Launfal as he tries—but ultimately fails—to keep this promise.

Another famous tale, *Sir Gawain and the Green Knight*, focuses on violence rather than love. This story concerns a bloody challenge between Gawain and an elf-like creature that wishes to behead him. This creature is green from head to toe and "terrible to behold, of stature greater than any on earth; from neck to loin so strong and thickly made, and with limbs so long and so great that he seemed even as a giant."[35]

The Green Knight is clearly a supernatural being not only because of his size and color but also because he continues to talk after Sir Gawain beheads him. These facts convince everyone present of the creature's mystical nature. "Many marvels had they seen, but none such as this, and phantasm and faërie did the folk deem it,"[36] the tale explains.

Less fantastic than the Green Knight but just as nasty is Morgan le Fay, the fairy villainess of Thomas Malory's 1485 work *Le Morte d'Arthur*. Morgan, whose last name means "the Fairy" in French, is King Arthur's half sister. She looks like a beautiful woman most of the time but also appears as an old hag, a wolf, a cow, and a crow. She lives on the fairy island of Avalon, where she works magical mischief on her royal brother and all the knights of his famous Round Table.

Shakespeare's Fairies

Mischief is also afoot in the works of William Shakespeare, a playwright who is sometimes described as the greatest writer in the

A Character Is Born

In traditional folklore the word *puck* was a generic term that referred to many types of fairies and sprites. In *A Midsummer Night's Dream*, however, William Shakespeare used this word as the name of a major character. Puck, or Robin Goodfellow, as the elf is also known, is clever and mischievous. Upon encountering the trickster, another fairy describes him with these words:

> Either I mistake your shape and making quite,
>
> Or else you are that shrewd and knavish sprite,
>
> Call'd Robin Goodfellow: are you not he
>
> That frights the maidens of the villagery;
>
> Skim milk; and sometimes labour in the quern,
>
> And bootless make the breathless housewife churn;
>
> And sometime make the drink to bear no barm;
>
> Mislead night-wanderers, laughing at their harm?
>
> Those that Hobgoblin call you, and sweet Puck,
>
> You do their work, and they shall have good luck:
>
> Are you not he?

This passage neatly sums up many folkloric traditions. It states, for example, that pucks frighten young women, steal milk, force housewives to churn, and lead travelers astray. By putting these traditions into writing, Shakespeare also cements the personality of this particular fairy. Puck is now a name, not just a word. As a result, the term *puck*, in its original sense, is now mostly forgotten outside of scholarly circles.

William Shakespeare, *A Midsummer Night's Dream*, act 2, scene 1, lines 32–42.

English language. Between the late 1500s and the early 1600s, Shakespeare produced dozens of plays and more than 150 sonnets. Many of these works touched on or even starred the Wee Folk.

This is particularly true of the play *A Midsummer Night's Dream*, a work that one critic says "contains the finest modern artistic realization of the fairy kingdom."[37] In this immensely popular tale, groups of fairies and humans gather in the woods one moonlit night to attend a wedding. A great deal of hilarious fairy trickery follows, much to the delight of audiences everywhere.

A Midsummer Night's Dream and other Shakespeare works are notable not just for their fairy characters but also for their joyful portrayals of the fairy folk. Although Shakespeare clearly had a deep understanding of the Little People, he tended to ignore the uglier aspects of these otherworldly beings. Instead, says one scholar, "he founded his elfin world on the prettiest of the people's traditions."[38] In Shakespeare's capable hands, fairies of all types assumed new and much more charming identities.

Shakespeare's elves offer a good example of this approach. One author describes these beings as follows: "The tiny elves, to whom a cowslip is tall, for whom the third part of a minute is an important division of time, have a miniature perfection which is charming. They delight in all beautiful and dainty things, and war with things that creep and things that fly, if they be uncomely; their lives are gay with fine frolic and delicate revelry."[39]

This portrayal was not exactly inaccurate, but it was definitely selective. It was also undeniably appealing. People loved Shakespeare's fairy folk—and they still do. Even today *A Midsummer Night's Dream* holds a special spot in the hearts of fairy lovers everywhere.

Titania and the fairies make flower garlands for the changeling baby in this illustration of a scene from William Shakespeare's A Midsummer Night's Dream. *Shakespeare portrays the fairy folk as joyful and charming.*

Fairy Tales

During the late 1600s a new type of fairy literature started to crop up. Instead of inventing original tales, writers now turned their attention to recording the old ones. The stories that came out of this effort are known as fairy tales. They are relatively modern summaries of centuries-old legends.

Charles Perrault and Madame d'Aulnoy were among the earliest writers to tackle this task. Both of these French authors published fairy-related collections in the final years of the 1600s. Perrault's work, titled *Tales and Stories of the Past with Morals: Tales of Mother Goose*, became particularly well known. It included the earliest written versions of "Cinderella," "Sleeping Beauty," and several other stories with fairy characters.

In the early 1800s the German brothers Jacob and Wilhelm Grimm expanded upon this effort. They collected 156 stories and published them in two volumes, one in 1812 and one in 1814. Not all of these stories concerned fairy folk, but many of them did. "The Elves and the Shoemaker" and "The Snow Queen," for example, described people's interactions with the fairy realm. By recording these stories and others, the Brothers Grimm hoped to preserve a fading part of their German culture.

A few decades later a Danish author named Hans Christian Andersen embarked on a similar task. Andersen penned nearly 170 fairy tales, many of which became immensely popular. One of these stories, "The Elf of the Rose," contains this delightful description of a tiny elf: "He was such a little wee thing, that no human eye could see him. . . . He was as well formed and as beautiful as a little child could be, and had wings that reached from his shoulders to his feet. . . . During the whole day he enjoyed himself in the warm sunshine, flew from flower to flower, and danced on the wings of the flying butterflies."[40]

> ## Did You Know?
>
> A statue of a mermaid based on Hans Christian Andersen's "The Little Mermaid" sits in the harbor of Copenhagen, Denmark. This famous fairy is said to guard ships that pass in and out.

Artistic Inspiration

Fairies do not just inspire writers and filmmakers. They are an endless source of material for artists as well. Over the centuries many famous paintings and illustrations have depicted elves and other types of fairies.

Some of these works are based on specific books, plays, or other writings. Shakespeare's *The Tempest*, for instance, features a fairy character named Ariel. This character appears in paintings by English artists Richard Dadd and Sir John Everett Millais. Paintings by other artists depict scenes from *A Midsummer Night's Dream*. Among these are *The Quarrel of Oberon and Titania* and *The Reconciliation of Oberon and Titania* by the nineteenth-century artist Sir Joseph Noel Paton. Paton's works hang today in the Scottish National Gallery for the public to enjoy. The books of J.M. Barrie, J.R.R. Tolkien, and many other authors have also inspired fairy artwork.

A great deal of original fairy-related art has also captured the public's attention. Painter Cicely Mary Barker, for example, became famous in the early to mid-1900s for her charming illustrations of flower fairies. These illustrations became the key element of a series of Flower Fairies books that included titles such as *Flower Fairies of the Spring* and *A Flower Fairy Alphabet*.

Author/illustrator Brian Froud has made a strong impression with his original illustrations as well. Froud's books include the classic *Faeries*, coauthored with Alan Lee, along with dozens of other works. Richly imagined and skillfully drawn, the illustrations from these books bring the denizens of Faericland to life.

Otherworldly Protectors

Despite his charming looks and habits, Andersen's elf is dangerous. He has the ability to whisper humans to their deaths. Not all fictional fairies, however, are so deadly. Many choose to help or protect people instead of harming them.

The fairy godmother is one such protector. These benevolent creatures pop up in many tales, the most famous of which is probably "Cinderella." In this story poor Cinderella cannot attend a ball because she has no way to get there and nothing to wear. A kind fairy saves the day by giving Cinderella magical clothing and transportation. First appearing in Perrault's 1697 collection, this story has been retold countless times by countless authors. It inspired the 1950 Disney film of the same name, which is surprisingly faithful to Perrault's original text.

The fairy-as-protector theme also appears in the work of a later author, Carlo Collodi. In the late 1800s Collodi's serial novel, titled *The Adventures of Pinocchio*, introduced a character called the fairy with the azure hair," a mother figure who tries to guide a marionette named Pinocchio in his quest to become human.

In Collodi's tale, the fairy's help comes mostly in the form of advice. The being does, however, bestow one great magical gift. Near the end of the book Pinocchio falls asleep after saving his father from certain death. The slumbering marionette dreams of his fairy friend, who says, "Bravo, Pinocchio! In reward for your kind heart, I forgive you for all your old mischief."[41] When Pinocchio awakes, he discovers that his dearest wish has come true: He has turned into a real human boy.

Like Perrault's "Cinderella," this tale also found new life in movie form. Disney's 1940 version of the story features the Blue Fairy, a tiny winged being with the power to grant wishes. People summon the fairy by wishing on stars. This element did not appear in Collodi's original work, but it turned out to be a popular twist. Thanks to Disney's *Pinocchio*, generations of fairy lovers now believe that "when you wish upon a star, your dreams come true."[42]

The Works of J.M. Barrie

Shortly after Collodi's *Pinocchio* appeared, another great work of fairy fiction made its debut. Scottish author J.M. Barrie's play *Peter Pan, or the Boy Who Wouldn't Grow Up* was staged for the first time in 1904. The play's plot concerned the ever-youthful Peter Pan and his fairy friend, Tinker Bell. Later adapted into a book called *Peter and Wendy*, this tale added several new conventions to the fairy canon.

One of these conventions concerned the origin of the fairy folk. Early in the book version of the story, Peter Pan explains to Wendy how fairies came into existence. "You see, Wendy, when the first baby laughed for the first time, its laugh broke into a thousand pieces, and they all went skipping about, and that was the beginning of fairies,"[43] he says.

In Barrie's imaginary world, children did not merely create fairies. They also have the ability to kill the Little People, albeit

The Blue Fairy visits Pinocchio in Disney's 1940 animated film. She eventually grants him his greatest wish: to be transformed from a marionette into a flesh-and-blood human boy.

unintentionally. Peter Pan also explains this fact to Wendy. "You see children know such a lot now, they soon don't believe in fairies, and every time a child says, 'I don't believe in fairies,' there is a fairy somewhere that falls down dead,"[44] he says.

Yet another invention that originated in Barrie's tales is a novel explanation for fairies' emotional natures. Barrie's Tinker Bell is a creature of extremes. Sometimes she is helpful and kind. At other times she is bad-tempered, cruel, and jealous. Barrie uses Tinker Bell's diminutive size to explain this fact. "Tink was not all bad: or, rather, she was all bad just now, but, on the other hand, sometimes she was all good. Fairies have to be one thing or the other, because being so small they unfortunately have room for one feeling only at a time,"[45] the author explains.

Peter and Wendy eventually made its way onto the big screen, following in the tradition of *Pinocchio* and *Cinderella*. Disney's 1953 adaptation of the story was called simply *Peter Pan*. This immensely popular film made Tinker Bell a household name. It also cemented Barrie's additions to the fairy tradition.

The Elves of J.R.R. Tolkien

Barrie's contributions are familiar to children in many parts of the world. Another renowned author, however, geared his inventions toward more sophisticated readers. An English writer named J.R.R. Tolkien turned his attention to fairies in general and elves in particular during the early to mid-1900s. Works including *The Hobbit* (1936), the *Lord of the Rings* trilogy (1954–55), and *The Silmarillion* (1977) described these beings' looks, habits, and abilities in painstaking detail. In doing so, they painted a picture that forever changed the way people viewed elves.

Among other things, Tolkien clearly specifies the elves' looks and physical form. Tolkien's elves are slender, a little bit taller than humans, and surpassingly beautiful. They are fair-skinned, and they have subtly pointed ears. Individuals of both sexes have long, flowing hair, although the males are beardless. All elves appear youthful and never seem to age, even though they are immortal and can actually be thousands of years old.

Tolkien's elves have a clear social structure to go with their distinct looks. These beings are divided into two major tribes and many minor ones. Each tribe has its own rulers, customs, and even its own language. They settle in communities with unique geographies and characteristics. The elfin outpost of Rivendell, for example, consists of several structures nestled among the foothills of the majestic Misty Mountains. Another community lives in Lórien (sometimes called Lothlórien), a remote forest that, explains one elf, "is the fairest of all the dwellings of my people."[46]

As lovely as it may be, Lórien and all other elfin settlements are conditional. They can only exist as long as the elves retain their magical powers. Even the elves themselves will fade away if their

J.R.R. Tolkien's beloved tales, along with popular elfin characters such as Legolas (pictured in the 2002 movie The Lord of the Rings: The Two Towers*), were slated to return to the big screen in two new movies— one in 2012 and the other in 2013.*

most powerful artifacts are destroyed. The elfin Lady Galadriel, who rules Lórien together with her husband, Lord Celeborn, explains this fact in one passage. "If you succeed [in destroying the ring], then our power is diminished, and Lothlórien will fade, and the tides of Time will sweep it away. We must depart into the West, or dwindle to a rustic folk of dell and cave, slowly to forget and to be forgotten,"[47] she says.

Passages like this one show how deeply Tolkien cared about his imaginary world. It is clear that the author carefully pondered elves and other mystical beings before setting pen to paper. The characters were alive in his mind; as a result, Tolkien was able to bring these beings to life with a depth and richness never before seen in any fictional work.

Bringing Tolkien to Film

Readers responded to Tolkien's efforts by snatching up his books, which became instant classics of the fantasy genre. *The Lord of the Rings* trilogy would eventually sell more than 150 million copies, making it one of the best-selling works of all time.

Considering this popularity, it is not surprising that Tolkien's masterpiece eventually made the leap to movie form. Like the original work, the film was released in three parts: *The Fellowship of the Ring* (2001), *The Two Towers* (2002), and *The Return of the King* (2003). Directed by Peter Jackson, this epic trilogy was a smashing commercial success, earning nearly $3 billion worldwide. The trilogy's final installment in particular was a critical smash as well. It won 11 Oscars, including the coveted Best Picture award. Impressively, the film captured every award for which it was nominated.

The trilogy's elves were undoubtedly part of the reason for this success. Filmmakers gave these beings every bit of the attention their original creator had lavished upon them, and the effort showed. Jackson gave his movie elves a carefully crafted appearance, distinctive clothing, and intricate dwellings. He hired top actors, including Orlando Bloom, Cate Blanchett, and Liv Tyler, to play the biggest elfin roles. He even hired a linguist to write Elvish dialogue for these actors, and he insisted that their lines must be delivered correctly. This work was not easy, but the result made it all worthwhile. "Now I'm glad that [Peter] insisted, because it sounds wonderful, and the Elvish language makes the story more beautiful and the feelings of our heroes more profound,"[48] Tyler said during a 2003 interview.

Fans will have at least two more chances to see this type of elfin magic at work. Again under the direction of Peter Jackson, *The Hobbit: An Unexpected Journey* is due to hit big screens in December 2012. The second half of the story, told in *The Hobbit: There and Back Again*, is scheduled to come out at the end of 2013. These films were to feature repeat appearances by the elf Legolas (played by Bloom), Lady Galadriel (played by Blanchett), and other favorite characters. For this reason and many others, Jackson's productions was sure to be welcome additions to the fairy canon.

Other Motion Pictures

Although few films can match the *Lord of the Rings* series in terms of clout, Wee Folk of various types have appeared in many other modern movies. One popular character is Dobby the House Elf, a brownie-like creature from J.K. Rowling's Harry Potter series. Introduced in the blockbuster books upon which the movies are based, Dobby is originally bound to the cruel Malfoy family. He is released from this bondage when Harry Potter tricks one of the Malfoys into giving Dobby a sock. "Master has presented Dobby with clothes! Dobby is free!"[49] the elf chortles before skittering off to begin his new life.

People who love the Harry Potter stories might also enjoy *Legend*. In this 1985 fantasy epic, a heroic human named Jack (played by Tom Cruise) must stop the villainous Lord of Darkness from casting the world into eternal night. Jack is joined on his quest by a fairy, an elf, and two dwarfs. The companions must overcome various obstacles before finding and subduing their evil foe.

In this film, mystical beings were the good guys. But fairy folk do not always fight evil. Sometimes they *are* the evil. One example of this usage is *Leprechaun*, a horror movie that came out in 1993. The film's plot concerns a sadistic leprechaun who stops at nothing, including murder, to retrieve his stolen pot of gold.

Leprechaun is undeniably cheesy. Still, it earned a cult following and eventually spawned five sequels. The most bewildering entry in the franchise is undoubtedly *Leprechaun 4: In Space* (1996), which tries to inject fairy lore into a science fiction/space travel/military plotline. It seems that not even fairy magic can make this combination work, however, because the film holds an approval rating of 0 percent on one popular movie-review site.

Enduring Popularity

This miserable rating, of course, has nothing to do with the film's leprechaun antagonist. Blockbusters like the *Lord of the Rings* films prove that moviegoers are still fascinated with the Little People. It is certain that moviemakers will continue to feed this fascination with new tales of the fairy realm.

Modern novelists, too, are continuing to pump original fairy-related stories into the marketplace. None of these novels have reached the prominence of the great fairy classics—yet. But there is no telling what the future may hold. Hundreds of years from now, some of the books being published today will undoubtedly be considered classic works of fairy fiction.

Chapter 4

Elves and Fairies in Popular Culture

Hundreds and even thousands of years ago, people around the world believed deeply in elves and other types of fairies. They felt sure that the fairy realm, although unseen, was just as real as the human world.

This belief has faded in modern times. People today tend to think of the Wee Folk as delightful but imaginary relics from a less sophisticated era. Despite this perception, however, people have not lost interest in the fairy world. On the contrary, they seem to be more fascinated by it than ever before. Fairies of all types now enjoy a robust existence in practically every aspect of modern popular culture.

The Tooth Fairy

The childhood tradition of the tooth fairy is one example of this trend. This tradition exists in many parts of the world, with the specifics varying slightly from place to place. In the Western version of the story, a fairy appears in the night to collect baby teeth shed by children. The fairy leaves money behind as payment for these objects.

The exact size, shape, and appearance of the tooth fairy are uncertain. Everyone has his or her own idea about this creature's looks. In a 1984 study, researcher (and, now, children's author) Rosemary Wells tried to quantify these ideas, but she came up with surprisingly scattershot results. "You've got your basic Tinkerbell-type tooth fairy with the wings, wand, a little older, and whatnot. Then you have some people who think of the tooth fairy as a man, or a bunny rabbit or a mouse,"[50] Wells explained in one interview.

Modern children's books have taken the concept even further. Illustrators have depicted the tooth fairy as a bear, a bat, a pixie, a dragon, a ballerina, and much more. On the editorial side, authors have invented entire tooth fairy cities, societies, rules, and motivations. There seems to be no end to the possible explanations for how and why the tooth fairy works her magic.

Should that be *her* magic—or perhaps *his*? The tooth fairy was undeniably, muscularly male in the 2010 film *Tooth Fairy*, a comedy that starred former pro wrestler Dwayne "the Rock" Johnson in the title role. In the film Johnson is magically sentenced to two weeks of tooth fairy duty as punishment for discouraging a child's hopes and dreams. The tall, burly Johnson has understandable trouble adapting to his new identity, which includes wings, a wand, and a pink tutu. He flies into plenty of walls and door frames before finally perfecting his job.

Holiday Cheer

No such practice is needed for the skilled craftsmen known far and wide as Santa's elves. These fairy folk are said to live with Santa Claus at the North Pole, where they work all year long building and stockpiling toys to be given as Christmas gifts. The elves are usually depicted as being short and slender, with pointy ears and noses. They can be either male or female. They usually dress in green tunics and hats. To these basic articles they add jingle bells, broad belts, colorful leggings, and other embellishments.

People have attributed many personality traits to Santa's elves. These beings are usually thought to be hardworking and serious on

The Fairy Doors of Ann Arbor

The college town of Ann Arbor, Michigan, seems to be a meeting point between the human and fairy worlds—or at least, that is what the city's famous "Fairy Doors" might lead viewers to believe. The Fairy Doors are tiny portals that appear overnight in the walls and door frames of public establishments. A peek through these doors reveals fairy-sized tables, chairs, dinnerware, and other objects.

During a 2006 interview, artist Jonathan Wright—who is suspected by some to be responsible for the Fairy Doors—expressed his thoughts on the fairies' settlement choices:

> The woodland, forest and flower fairies had been living in nature but were being displaced by urban sprawl. Searching for a new domicile, the winged ones . . . ventured into Ann Arbor. . . . Liking what they saw, they decided to uproot to specific addresses amenable to fairies. . . .
>
> The urban fairies have clear favorites. Judging by the locations of the doors, and by the items sold in the related stores, they enjoy toys, art, candy, fashion, deli meats, theater and caffeine. . . . They may also have a yen for books and chocolate.
>
> No one has ever reported seeing an actual fairy behind one of the Fairy Doors. This fact, however, does not affect the popularity of the diminutive doors. Beloved by adults and children alike, these mysterious installations have become icons of the Ann Arbor pop culture scene.

Andrea Sachs, "Ann Arbor Proudly Presents: The Doors," *Washington Post*, April 23, 2006. www.washingtonpost.com.

the job but jolly and fun-loving when the workday is over. They are devoted to Santa Claus and will gladly do anything the big boss asks. This attachment is so deep that it borders on a parent/child relationship. "Santa loves all the elves equally; they're like his children,"[51] explains one author.

People love Santa's elves, too. They love them so much, in fact, that the North Pole elves have earned a prominent role in the Western Christmas tradition. People hang elf ornaments on their Christmas trees and place elf dolls on their mantels. They read storybooks about elves and write letters to them. Thanks to modern technology, they can even become elves—virtually, anyway. The immensely popular JibJab.com application known as *ElfYourself* places people's uploaded headshots onto the bodies of dancing, singing elves. Funny and free, *ElfYourself* claims to have spawned nearly 500 million customized elves since its debut in 2006.

Less personal but equally beloved are the many Christmas elf–related offerings that have made their way to movie screens. Comedies such as *The Santa Clause* (1994), starring Tim Allen as Santa, and *Elf* (2003), starring Will Ferrell as a human raised by elves, have become holiday classics. Elves also play a prominent role in the 2011 animated film *Arthur Christmas*, which focuses on the title character's frantic effort to deliver a forgotten Christmas gift. Thanks to a little elfish assistance, Arthur succeeds in his quest.

Making the Leap to Television

Christmas elves do not populate only the big screen. They have popped up in many television offerings as well. The best loved of these offerings may be the 1964 stop-action classic *Rudolph the Red-Nosed Reindeer*, which features an elf named Hermey as one of its central characters. Hermey is different from his North Pole colleagues because he wants to be a dentist instead of a toymaker. Initially the other elves ridicule Hermey for this desire. By the end of the film, though, Hermey has earned his friends' respect and is able to open the dental office of his dreams.

In more recent years, an animated Christmas special called *Prep & Landing* has brought another vision of Santa's helpers to life. This award-winning tale concerns an elite group of elves who prepare human homes for Santa's arrival. The soldier-style elves check to make sure everyone is asleep, trim Christmas trees to make room for gifts, preopen stockings, and even install lighted landing strips on roof tops. By doing these things, the elves ensure that Santa's visits are smooth and error-free.

Prep & Landing showcases the technical expertise of the Little People. Other television productions, however, take a much lighter approach. The popular Nickelodeon cartoon series *The Fairly Odd-Parents*, for instance, is about a boy named Timmy who has two fairy godparents. The fairies grant Timmy's every wish, with predictably disastrous results.

Another well-known television fairy is named Abby Cadabby. Part of the *Sesame Street* franchise, Abby is a three-year-old fairy

In the 1964 Christmas classic, Rudolph the Red-Nosed Reindeer, *Hermey the elf aspires to be a dentist rather than a toymaker. He is ridiculed by his fellow elves but eventually wins their respect and achieves his dream.*

in training. Pink, puffy, and pretty, she is endlessly astonished by the mysteries of human reading, writing, and arithmetic. "That's so magical!" Abby exclaims whenever she learns something new.

Abby Cadabby is not the only fairy character aimed at young children. Many others appear in various shows and series around the world. These characters may be a bit too sweet for the serious fairy lover's taste, but they serve an important purpose nonetheless. They introduce a whole new generation of children to the fairy world in a format they can understand and enjoy.

Wee Salesfolk

Fairy-related television commercials—especially those that promote child-friendly products—can do the same thing. This usage makes sense. Tradition, after all, says that fairies can use their powers of glamour to make humans see and believe anything they wish. It seems that this ability would make fairies very good salesfolk.

This is certainly true of the Keebler Elves. This band of merry animated bakers has been living and working inside a hollowed-out tree since 1968, when the elves were introduced. Most famously responsible for E.L. Fudge cookies, the Keebler Elves are among the most popular advertising icons of all time. They are a major part of Keebler's brand image to this day.

Kellogg's Snap, Crackle, and Pop are equally recognizable. These cheerful elves (or, some say, gnomes) have hawked Rice Krispies cereal since the 1930s. They have appeared not only on cereal boxes but also in print ads and television cartoons. The elves' names represent the sound Rice Krispies make when immersed in milk. "Snap! Crackle! Pop!" the elves exclaim in a simple yet catchy phrase that inspires visions of breakfast for generations of television viewers.

Breakfast might not be the first thing on a sports fan's mind during football season. At these times, viewers' thoughts turn toward

> ## Did You Know?
>
> The 2004 film *The Polar Express* depicts one of the largest gatherings of North Pole elves ever to appear on the big screen. In this movie, countless thousands of these beings gather to cheer Santa off on his Christmas Eve journey.

Mrs. Claus Explains the Elves

Children around the world ask questions about Santa's elves each year when Christmastime rolls around. In 2011 a Finnish website published what it described as an interview with Mrs. Claus that attempted to answer some of these questions.

Are new elves still being born?

New Christmas elves and other kinds of elves are born frequently. When the last rays of the evening sun meet with the Northern Lights, the wind is blowing from the north and the stars are shining, that is when elves are born. . . .

What do Santa and his elves do during their free time?

They play lots of games. One of their favorite things to do is sit by the fireplace and talk about everything in the world. They reminisce about past journeys and recall interesting people and places that they have visited through the years.

Can humans see elves?

Elves are good at sneaking around, so it's usually hard to detect them. Children are often able to see a branch move, or notice something looking through the window or peeping from behind the curtains. Then they know that it's their own personal elf tiptoeing around. Sometimes elves move something or leave some other sign to show that they have been around. They have also been known to pick up mail addressed to Santa Claus.

Heli Karjalainen and Annikki Marjala, "Exclusive Interview: Mrs. Claus," This Is Finland, 2011. http://finland.fi.

the big game and how they plan to watch it. The hilarious Football Fairy has the answer to this question. Played by professional football player Deion Sanders, the Football Fairy is tiny, winged, and dressed in a white football uniform. He impatiently educates sports fans about the merits of DirecTV by flinging magical fireballs that transform the televised sports experience.

The Disney Fairies Franchise

Fairy folk may have a proven ability to sell products. In terms of sheer numbers, however, one modern offering clearly flits head and wings above the rest. The Disney Fairies franchise, which was launched by the Walt Disney Company in 2005, is a promotional vehicle that stars Peter Pan's fairy friend, Tinker Bell. Popular from the beginning, this franchise quickly grew into a multibillion-dollar property that now includes books, movies, a website, clothing, toy tie-ins, and much more.

This success was no surprise to Disney executives. They knew that fairies were just as popular as ever. They also knew that many adults had fond childhood memories of Tinker Bell. By combining these facts with an original approach, Disney expected to create something magical for modern children. "Certainly the nostalgia and familiarity that parents have with Tinker Bell is going to help. Then there's the fresh new creativity that will make it relevant for today's kids,"[52] said one Disney official just before the franchise's launch.

The "fresh new creativity" that this official mentions is, in reality, a significant creative effort. Tinker Bell has been fully fleshed out in her newest incarnation. She has a history, a distinct personality, friends, enemies, and even a job—she is a "tinker-talent" fairy, responsible for fixing pots and pans. Tink, as she is affectionately known, lives in a magical community in the heart of Never Land. Pixie Hollow, as the fairies' home is called, is the backdrop for many events that occur in the franchise's fictional offerings.

> # Did You Know?
>
> In November 2009 Tinker Bell became the smallest waxwork ever to be made at Madame Tussaud's wax museum. The tiny figure was only 5.5 inches (14cm) tall.

These offerings have established a proven track record of success among their target audience. Young girls seem to adore the Disney Fairies, and they continue to snatch up whatever new products the franchise offers. They embrace each new opportunity to immerse themselves in the fairy realm.

Role-Playing Games

It seems that many adults feel the same way. The gaming market offers several fairy-themed role-playing games that let players create their own characters and story lines. Enduringly popular, these games give mere mortals a taste of the fairy existence.

One of the best-known fairies is Disney's Tinker Bell, who appears here in a scene from the 1953 animated film Peter Pan. *In her more recent incarnation, she has a distinct personality and is affectionately known as Tink.*

White Wolf Gaming Studio's *Changeling: The Dreaming* was the first major offering in this genre. This game was part of White Wolf's World of Darkness line, which was published and sold from 1991 to 2004. Its premise revolves around beings called changelings. These changelings are not abducted humans in the usual sense of the word; rather, they are fairy souls reborn into human bodies. Players follow the conceptual guidelines of the story to develop unique characters. These characters then interact with others to create original situations and story lines.

In 2004 White Wolf retired its original World of Darkness line and replaced it with a new series of games. The New World of Darkness included a totally revised and much darker version of *Changeling* that has proven to be even more popular than the original. Called *Changeling: The Lost*, this product sticks much more closely to the classic concept of changelings. It paints the picture of a scary world where otherworldly creatures regularly abduct mortals and whisk them away to another plane of existence. Time is different in this realm, so centuries can pass while the fairies toy with their human captives. For most people, this torture goes on forever. A determined few, however, are able to escape. They break through the fairies' defenses and return to the mortal world—only to discover that everything has changed. As the game's developer states, "The families and friends are either long gone, have forgotten them, or have never realized they were missing—because something else took their place. These hapless mortals, touched irrevocably by Glamour, are the Lost."[53]

This premise is creepy but undeniably fascinating, just as many people imagine the fairy realm itself to be. Seductive in its scariness, *Changeling* lets gamers explore the darker side of the fairy tradition.

Fairy Gardens

This sinister approach does not suit everyone. Many people prefer to envision the fairy world as a place of sweetness and light. They like the traditional view of gentle, winged Wee Folk who flit like ethereal butterflies from flower to flower, sometimes befriending humans along the way.

For people who feel this way, the modern hobby of fairy gardening may be a pleasant diversion. Fairy gardens are outdoor havens designed specifically to attract flower fairies. Bursting with fairy-friendly objects and plants, these retreats just might give their creators the chance to spot fairy folk in action.

A good fairy garden should have several key elements. Perhaps most importantly, it should have plenty of places where tiny beings can take shelter. "Be sure to include fairy houses, flowering shrubs, gnarled tree stumps and rock outcroppings in your miniature garden to entice fairies to settle. . . . Fairies will want a place to hide and will tend to make their home in gardens that provide outlets to quickly disappear from the prying attention of human eyes,"[54] one website explains.

Fairy gardens should also include certain plants that are known to be fairy favorites. The fairy folk particularly love cowslips and sometimes choose to live within their petals. They like pansies, primroses, and heather as well, and they cannot resist the sweet scent of roses and wild thyme. A weed called ragwort may also be a welcome addition to one's garden because fairies use the stems of this plant like witches' brooms to fly through the air.

Along with these desirable plants, there are a few that should never be used. Bluebells in particular will place the human gardener in great danger. "To hear the ring of a Bluebell is to hear one's death knell. . . . A bluebell wood is an extremely hazardous place to be—a place of faerie-woven spells and enchantments,"[55] say folklorists Brian Froud and Alan Lee.

Other plants should be avoided not because they are dangerous but simply because they repel fairies. Four-leaf clovers and Saint-John's-wort both fall into this category. These plants are said to break fairies' spells or to provide other protections against the Wee Folk, and fairies will not settle in places where they grow. Even the prettiest fairy garden will therefore fail if it contains these offensive flora.

Living like Elves and Fairies

The creation of a fairy garden is an attempt, perhaps not entirely serious, to attract actual fairies. But not everyone wants to engage in this type of work or, indeed, even to see ethereal beings. They would rather express their love for the fairy realm by decorating their homes in a fairy-like manner.

This approach is especially common when it comes to little girls' rooms. Furniture, bedding, artwork, books, toys, clocks, and countless other fairy-themed objects have been used to transform many a plain room into an otherworldly wonderland—proof positive of the fairy's impact on modern culture.

Well hidden within the flowering shrubs and rocky outcroppings of a fairy garden, shy fairies mourn the passing of a kindred spirit—a bird. Fairies might befriend a human but are more likely to form a bond with nature's other creatures.

Mere decorations, however, are not enough for true fairy enthusiasts. Some people feel so connected to the fairy realm that they actually want to live in fairy dwellings. They build or renovate homes to specifications that fulfill this desire. One such dwelling is a Wales residence created by Simon Dale and his wife, Jasmine Saville. This home looks like something straight out of a movie. The dwelling is built entirely of natural woodland materials. It is small, rounded, and partly buried in a hillside. Pictures of the house's interior reveal a snug space with tilted walls, a sloped roof, and wooden accents everywhere. Any fairy being would be right at home in this magical abode.

The couple acknowledge that their house is unusual, but they like it. "The aesthetic appeals to lots of people and perhaps touches something innate in us that evolved in forests,"[56] says Saville. Living in their fairy-inspired home, this family certainly feels closer to the natural world around them.

A Spiritual Side

This type of connection can be hard to find in modern times. As the world has gotten more industrial, people have become more and more removed from nature. Many people are deeply unhappy with this situation and are trying to change it. Fairies, they believe, can show them how to accomplish this task.

A belief system called the Faerie Faith operates on this principle. People who practice this philosophy believe in fairies and view them as a type of spiritual guide. In the larger picture, adherents regard nature as a life force with many aspects. One of these aspects, of course, is the fairy realm. "There should be a sensitivity, a belief, of the spiritual reality behind what we refer to as Nature. There should be a sincere love of Earth Herself and a desire to communicate with her other children. There should be a belief in the individual life of this planet, and a certainty that it permeates the whole world,"[57] reads a statement of the Faerie Faith's tenets.

Followers of the Faerie Faith take a serious, almost religious approach to fairy contact. Other people, however, do not see the need for these types of rules and regulations. There is a general belief among fairy enthusiasts that regular folks can commune with the Little People. They simply need to follow a few commonsense steps. These steps usually involve going to certain places at certain times of the day, month, or year. When these external conditions are right, people simply need to make themselves receptive to the fairy influence. Then, like magic, the Wee Folk will appear.

The definition of *receptive* varies from person to person. Some people recommend reciting charms or ingesting certain plants, such as harebells and primroses. Others suggest that it is helpful to meditate or immerse oneself in a creative activity. These activities might distract a person from the "real" world just long enough to let the fairy realm slip through.

One fact is consistent among nearly all sources. It seems that however a person chooses to approach fairies, he or she should do it in a positive frame of mind. This is because pleasant humans are much more likely to succeed in their quest for fairy encounters. One website devoted to fairies explains this concept: "Just like humans, fairies are more attracted to lightness and happiness rather than sadness and depression. In fact, much that has been written about fairies has to do with them playing music, dancing, singing and basically partying all night. When you are trying to attract them, try playing beautiful music, dance a little and feel happy!"[58]

Following this advice does not guarantee that a person will see fairies, but it is sound advice nonetheless. Any activity that puts a person into a calm, happy, or joyful mood is good for the soul. Even if a fairy-summoning fails, seeking these beings is therefore always worthwhile.

In Love with Fairies

This is no revelation to the countless millions or perhaps even billions of people around the world who adore fairies. It is fun to read about fairies, to watch them in the movies and on television, to draw and paint them, to do jigsaw puzzles bearing their pictures, and much more. It is even fun to dress like the Little Folk. Many children—and adults, too—happily "become" Tinker Bell, the tooth fairy, a Christmas elf, or other types of fairy folk on Halloween and other dress-up occasions.

These activities and myriad others show how deeply the fairy tradition has permeated modern popular culture. People today may not realize that they are perpetuating ancient legends when they don, say, a T-shirt bearing an image of a fairy, but they are. Through the simplest everyday acts, people everywhere keep the idea of elves and all other types of fairies alive.

Source Notes

Introduction: All in the Family

1. J.R.R. Tolkien, "The Ring Goes South," book 2, chap. 3, *The Fellowship of the Ring.* New York: HarperCollins e-books, 2009. http://books.google.com.

2. Tolkien, "The Ring Goes South," book 2, chap. 3, *The Fellowship of the Ring.*

3. Brian Froud and Alan Lee, "A Note on the Use of the Word F-A-E-R-I-E," in *Faeries.* New York: Peacock/Bantam, 1978.

Chapter One: Defining Elves and Fairies

4. Pierre Dubois, *The Great Encyclopedia of Fairies.* New York: Simon and Schuster, 2000, p. 12.

5. Brian Froud, preface to *Good Faeries, Bad Faeries.* New York: Simon and Schuster, 1998.

6. Jacob Grimm, "Wights and Elves," in *Teutonic Mythology,* vol. 2, chap. 17, trans. James Steven Stallybrass. London: George Bell & Sons, 1883. www.archive.org.

7. Grimm, *Teutonic Mythology.*

8. John Brand, *A New Description of Orkney: Zetland, Pightland-Firth, and Caithness.* 1703. http://books.google.co.uk.

9. Rasmus B. Anderson and George Stephens, trans., "Here Begins the Saga of Thorstein, Viking's Son," chap. 1, *Viking Tales of the North: The Sagas of Thorstein, Viking's Son, and Fridthjof the Bold; also, Tegner's Fridthjof's Saga.* 1901. Reprint, Whitefish, MT: Kessinger, 2008. www.northvegr.org.

10. Froud and Lee, "The Realm of Faerie," in *Faeries.*

11. Philip Carr-Gomm and Richard Heygate, *The Book of English Magic.* New York: Penguin, 2010. http://books.google.com.

12. Santharian Dream, "The Elven Race (Styreians)." www.san tharia.com.

13. Francis Melville, *The Book of Faeries*. Hauppage, NY: Barron's, 2002, p. 78.

14. Quoted in W.Y. Evans-Wentz, *The Fairy-Faith in Celtic Countries*.1911. Reprint, New York: Lemma, 1973, p. 47.

15. Palmer Cox, "The Origin of the 'Brownies,'" *Ladies' Home Journal*, November 1892. www.brownie-camera.com.

16. Monstrous.com, "Fairy Powers," 2011. www.monstrous.com.

17. Snorri Sturluson, *Edda,* trans. Anthony Faulkes. Rutland, VT: Charles E. Tuttle, 1995.

Chapter Two: Encounters with the Little People

18. Janet Bord, *Fairies: Real Encounters with Little People*. New York: Carroll & Graf, 1997, p. 1.

19. Froud, "Pixies," in *Good Fairies, Bad Fairies*.

20. Andrew Lang, *The Blue Fairy Book*. New York: Dover, 1965, p. 274.

21. Lang, *The Blue Fairy Book*, p. 276.

22. Froud and Lee, "Pixies," in *Faeries*.

23. Thomas Keightley, "Elves," in *The Fairy Mythology*. London: H.G. Bohn, 1870. www.sacred-texts.com.

24. Froud and Lee, "Faerie Ways," in *Faeries*.

25. Keightley, "The Changeling," in *The Fairy Mythology*.

26. Katharine Mary Briggs, *An Encyclopedia of Fairies*. New York: Pantheon, 1976, p. 41.

27. Keightley, "The Leprechaun in the Garden," in *The Fairy Mythology*.

28. W. Jenkyn Thomas, "The Fairy Wife," in *The Welsh Fairy Book*. 1907. Reprint, Whitefish, MT: Kessinger, 2004.

29. V.U. Hammershaimb, "Kópakonan: The Legend of the Seal-Woman," trans. A.E. Petersen, 1891.www.tjatsi.fo.

30. Bord, foreword to *Fairies*.

31. Quoted in Bord, *Fairies*, p. 5.

Chapter Three: Elves and Fairies in Literature and Film

32. Jennifer Holm, trans., "Tam Lin." Tam Lin Balladry: Versions. www.tam-lin.org.

33. Tam Lin Balladry: Tales, "Comparing 'Tam Lin' to 'Thomas the Rhymer,'" www.tam-lin.org.

34. Quoted in Thomas Chestre, "Sir Launfal," in *"Harken to Me": Middle English Romances in Translation*, trans. George W. Tuma and Dinah Hazell. New York: W.W. Norton, 1995. www.sfsu.edu.

35. Jessie L. Weston, trans., "Sir Gawain and the Green Knight," Camelot Project at the University of Rochester. www.lib.rochester.edu.

36. Weston, "Sir Gawain and the Green Knight."

37. T.F. Thiselton Dyer, *Folk-Lore of Shakespeare*. New York: Harper & Brothers, 1884, p. 1. www.sacred-texts.com.

38. Quoted in Dyer, *Folk-Lore of Shakespeare*.

39. Quoted in Dyer, *Folk-Lore of Shakespeare*.

40. Hans Christian Andersen, "The Elf of the Rose," Hans Christian Andersen Fairy Tales and Stories. http://hca.gilead.org.il.

41. Carlo Collodi, *The Adventures of Pinocchio*, Project Gutenberg. www.gutenberg.org.

42. *Pinocchio*. Directed by Ben Sharpsteen and Hamilton Luske. Walt Disney Productions, 1940.

43. J.M. Barrie, *Peter and Wendy*. New York: Charles Scribner's Sons, 1911, p. 43.

44. Barrie, *Peter and Wendy*, p. 43.

45. Barrie, *Peter and Wendy*, pp. 74–75.

46. Tolkien, "Lothlórien," book 2, chap. 6, *The Fellowship of the Ring*.

47. Tolkien, "The Mirror of Galadriel," book 2, chap. 7, *The Fellowship of the Ring*.

48. Quoted in Lovely Liv Tyler Website, "I'm Not an Elf. Although I'm Not So Sure Anymore," *Calendar Magazine*, January/February 2003, p. 12. www.lovelylivtyler.com.

49. *Harry Potter and the Chamber of Secrets*. Directed by Chris Columbus. Warner Bros. Pictures, 2002.

Chapter Four: Elves and Fairies in Popular Culture

50. Quoted in Meg Kissinger, "The Tooth Fairy: Friend or Foe?," *Milwaukee Journal*, July 31, 1991, p. A2.

51. Northpole.com, "Question & Answer with Santa," January 2012. www.northpole.com.

52. Quoted in Laura Petrecca, "Disney Hopes Fairies Will Fly into Girls' Hearts," *USA Today Online*, August 25, 2005. www.usa today.com.

53. White Wolf, World of Darkness, World of Darkness Wiki, December 18, 2011. wiki.white-wolf.com.

54. Enchanted Gardens, "How to Attract Fairies into Your Miniature Garden," 2012. www.miniature-gardens.com.

55. Froud and Lee, "Faerie Flora," in *Faeries*.

56. Jasmine Saville, "At Home in the Forest," A Low Impact Woodland Home. http://simondale.net.

57. Linda Kerr, "What Is the Faerie Faith?," Linda's Faerie Faith Page, July 24, 2003. www.faeriefaith.net.

58. Natalie Lynn, "How to Attract Fairies," Real Fairies, October 31, 2008. www.realfairies.net.

For Further Exploration

Nonfiction Books

Nancy Arrowsmith, *Field Guide to the Little People: A Curious Journey into the Hidden Realm of Elves, Faeries, Hobgoblins & Other Not-So-Mythical Creatures*. Woodbury, MN: Llewellyn, 2009.

Brian Froud and Alan Lee, *Faeries*. New York: Abrams, 2010.

Stephen D. Rogers, *The Dictionary of Made-Up Languages: From Adunaic to Elvish, Zaum to Klingon—the Anwa (Real) Origins of Invented Lexicons*. Avon, MA: Adams Media, 2011.

Fiction Books

Hans Christian Andersen, *The Complete Hans Christian Andersen Fairy Tales*. New York: Gramercy, 2006.

J.M. Barrie, *Peter Pan—the Original*. London: Vintage Classic, 2009.

Carlo Collodi, *Pinocchio*. New York: Knopf, 2011.

Jacob Grimm and Wilhelm Grimm, *Grimm's Complete Fairy Tales*. San Diego: Canterbury Classics, 2011.

James Napoli, *The North Pole Employee Handbook: A Guide to Policies, Rules, Regulations and Daily Operations for the Worker at North Pole Industries*. Kennebunkport, ME: Cider Mill, 2008.

J.R.R. Tolkien, *The Fellowship of the Ring: The Lord of the Rings, Part One*. New York: Mariner, 2012.

J.R.R. Tolkien, *The Hobbit*. New York: Mariner, 2012.

J.R.R. Tolkien, *The Return of the King: The Lord of the Rings, Part Three*. New York: Mariner Books, 2012.

J.R.R. Tolkien, *The Two Towers: The Lord of the Rings, Part Two*. New York: Mariner, 2012.

Websites

The Cottingley Network (www.cottingley.net). Every aspect of the Cottingley Fairies controversy is examined on this comprehensive site.

A Low Impact Woodland Home (http://simondale.net). This site includes background information on the concept, design, and construction of Simon Dale's delightful Hobbit House as well as photos of similar homes around the world.

Monstrous (www.monstrous.com). This site has extensive information on every imaginable mythical creature, including elves and fairies.

One Wiki to Rule Them All (http://lotr.wikia.com). This publicly edited site offers more than 4,000 encyclopedia-style entries about the people, place, events, and beings in Tolkien's *Lord of the Rings* trilogy.

Project Gutenberg (www.gutenberg.org). This website offers free full-text versions of more than 100,000 classic works, including many that concern the fairy folk.

Index

Note: Bold page numbers indicate illustrations.

Picture Credits

Cover: Thinkstock/Hemera

© Christie's Images/Corbis: 11, 19

The Fairie's Banquet, 1859 (oil on canvas), Fitzgerald, John Anster (1832-1906)/Fairy Art Museum, Tokyo, Japan/The Bridgeman Art Library: 64

Kharbine-Tapabor/The Art Archive at Art Resource, NY: 42

Midsummer Eve (w/c heightened with gouache on paper), Hughes, Edward Robert (1851-1914)/Private Collection/Photo © Christie's Images/The Bridgeman Art Library: 25

Photofest: 7, 47, 49, 57, 61

© Swim Inc 2, LLC/Corbis: 34

About the Author

Kris Hirschmann has written more than 200 books for children. She owns and runs a business that provides a variety of writing and editorial services. She lives near Orlando, Florida, with her husband, Michael, and her daughters, Nikki and Erika.